Method Description, Quality Assurance, Environmental Data, and other Information for Analysis of Pharmaceuticals in Wastewater-Treatment-Plant Effluents, Streamwater, and Reservoirs, 2004-2009

Open-File Report 2010–1102

U.S. Department of the Interior
U.S. Geological Survey

science for a changing world

Prepared in cooperation with the
New York State Department of Environmental Conservation

Method Description, Quality Assurance, Environmental Data, and other Information for Analysis of Pharmaceuticals in Wastewater-Treatment-Plant Effluents, Streamwater, and Reservoirs, 2004-2009

By Patrick J. Phillips, Steven G. Smith, Dana W. Kolpin, Steven D. Zaugg, Herbert T. Buxton, and Edward T. Furlong

Open-File Report 2010–1102

U.S. Department of the Interior
U.S. Geological Survey

U.S. Department of the Interior
KEN SALAZAR, Secretary

U.S. Geological Survey
Marcia K. McNutt, Director

U.S. Geological Survey, Reston, Virginia 2010

For product and ordering information:
World Wide Web: http://www.usgs.gov/pubprod
Telephone: 1-888-ASK-USGS

For more information on the USGS—the Federal source for science about the Earth,
its natural and living resources, natural hazards, and the environment:
World Wide Web: http://www.usgs.gov
Telephone: 1-888-ASK-USGS

Contents

Figures

Graphs showing:

Tables

Conversion Factors

Multiply	By	To obtain
Length		
centimeter (cm)	0.3937	inch (in.)
millimeter (mm)	0.03937	inch (in.)
meter (m)	3.281	foot (ft)
kilometer (km)	0.6214	mile (mi)
Volume		
liter (L)	33.82	ounce, fluid (fl. oz)
liter (L)	0.2642	gallon (gal)
Flow rate		
cubic meter per second (m^3/s)	35.31	cubic foot per second (ft^3/s)
liter per second (L/s)	15.85	gallon per minute (gal/min)
cubic foot per second (ft^3/s)	0.02832	cubic meter per second (m^3/s)

Temperature in degrees Celsius (°C) may be converted to degrees Fahrenheit (°F) as follows:
°F=(1.8×°C)+32
Temperature in degrees Fahrenheit (°F) may be converted to degrees Celsius (°C) as follows:
°C=(°F-32)/1.8
Specific conductance is given in microsiemens per centimeter at 25 degrees Celsius (µS/cm at 25°C).
Concentrations of chemical constituents in water are given either in milligrams per liter (mg/L) or micrograms per liter (µg/L).

Abbreviations

CASRN	CAS Registry Number®
FDA	U.S. Food and Drug Administration
GC	Gas chromatography
MDL	Method detection limit
MS	Mass spectrometry
NIH	U.S. National Institutes of Health
PFF	Pharmaceutical formulation facility
PMF	Pharmaceutical manufacturing facility
PPF	Pharmaceutical production facility
RPD	Relative percent difference
RSD	Relative standard deviation
SPE	Solid-phase extraction
TIC	Tentatively identified compounds
USGS	U.S. Geological Survey
WWTP	Wastewater treatment plant

Method Description, Quality Assurance, Environmental Data, and other Information for Analysis of Pharmaceuticals in Wastewater-Treatment-Plant Effluents, Streamwater, and Reservoirs, 2004-2009.

By Patrick J. Phillips, Steven G. Smith, Dana W. Kolpin, Steven D. Zaugg, Herbert T. Buxton, and Edward T. Furlong

Abstract

Wastewater-treatment-plant (WWTP) effluents are a demonstrated source of pharmaceuticals to the environment. During 2004-09, a study was conducted to identify pharmaceutical compounds in effluents from WWTPs (including two that receive substantial discharges from pharmaceutical formulation facilities), streamwater, and reservoirs. The methods used to determine and quantify concentrations of seven pharmaceuticals are described. In addition, the report includes information on pharmaceuticals formulated or potentially formulated at the two pharmaceutical formulation facilities that provide substantial discharge to two of the WWTPs, and potential limitations to these data are discussed. The analytical methods used to provide data on the seven pharmaceuticals (including opioids, muscle relaxants, and other pharmaceuticals) in filtered water samples also are described. Data are provided on method performance, including spike data, method detection limit results, and an estimation of precision. Quality-assurance data for sample collection and handling are included. Quantitative data are presented for the seven pharmaceuticals in water samples collected at WWTP discharge points, from streams, and at reservoirs. Occurrence data also are provided for 19 pharmaceuticals that were qualitatively identified. Flow data at selected WWTP and streams are presented.

Between 2004-09, 35-38 effluent samples were collected from each of three WWTPs in New York and analyzed for seven pharmaceuticals. Two WWTPs (NY2 and NY3) receive substantial inflows (greater than 20 percent of plant flow) from pharmaceutical formulation facilities (PFF) and one (NY1) receives no PFF flow. Samples of effluents from 23 WWTPs across the United States were analyzed once for these pharmaceuticals as part of a national survey. Maximum pharmaceutical effluent concentrations for the national survey and NY1 effluent samples were generally less than 1 µg/L. Four pharmaceuticals (methadone, oxycodone, butalbital and metaxalone) in samples of NY3 effluent had median concentrations ranging from 3.4 to greater than 400 µg/L. Maximum concentrations of oxycodone (1,700 µg/L) and metaxalone (3,800 µg/L) in samples from NY3 effluent exceeded 1,000 µg/L. Three pharmaceuticals (butalbital, carisoprodol, and oxycodone) in samples of NY2 effluent had median concentrations ranging from 2 to 11 µg/L. These findings suggest that current manufacturing practices at these PFFs can result in pharmaceutical concentrations from 10 to 1,000 times higher than those typically found in WWTP effluents.

Introduction

Over the last decade, numerous studies have documented the occurrence of pharmaceuticals in streams (Ashton and others, 2004; Bruchet and others, 2005; Kim and others, 2007; and Kolpin and others, 2002) and have identified wastewater treatment plants (WWTPs) as a major source of pharmaceuticals to the environment (Ternes and others, 1999; Clara and others, 2005; Glassmeyer and others, 2005; Karthikeyan and Meyer, 2006; Vieno and others, 2007; Chang and others, 2007, Ying and others, 2009). The long-term effects of low-level exposure to complex mixtures of pharmaceuticals on stream biota are poorly understood, although a variety of potential adverse effects have been documented at these low levels, including acute and chronic damage to biota (Quinn and others, 2008; Crane and others, 2006), accumulation in tissues (Brooks and others, 2003; Paterson and Metcalfe, 2008), reproductive damage (Nentwig, 2007), inhibition of cell proliferation (Pomati and others, 2006), and behavioral changes (Stanley and others, 2007; Gaworecki and Klaine, 2008). Continued research to identify and quantify pharmaceuticals in susceptible environmental settings and to identify potential effects on the ecology in those settings is essential for the future protection of water quality and ecological health.

The discharges from facilities that manufacture pharmaceutical products are an under-investigated source of pharmaceuticals to the environment; only limited data are currently (2010) available worldwide. Pharmaceutical manufacturing facilities (PMFs) include pharmaceutical production facilities (PPFs), which produce active pharmaceutical ingredients, and pharmaceutical formulation facilities (PFFs), which formulate and package pharmaceutical products (Hoerger and others, 2009). Past studies of pharmaceutical sources to the environment have focused on consumer use and disposal, and hospital waste (Brooks and others, 2003; Heberer and Feldmann, 2005; Watkinson and others, 2009). However, a study in India (Larsson and others, 2007) found antibiotic concentrations as high as 31,000 µg/L (micrograms per liter) in WWTP effluent that receives substantial discharges from several PPFs, and these discharges have resulted in pharmaceutical concentrations of 1,000 µg/L in nearby groundwater and surface water (Fick and others, 2009). Similarly, diclofenac concentrations exceeded 20 µg/L in effluent from a WWTP in Taiwan receiving PPF discharge (Lin and others, 2008). These concentrations are orders of magnitude higher than typical concentrations reported for WWTP effluents in the United States and Europe (generally below 1 µg/L).

This report is a companion report to Phillips and others (2010), which (1) describes the occurrence of 11 opioids, muscle relaxants, and other pharmaceuticals in effluents from 23 WWTPs across the United States collected between 2006-2009, (2) compares the concentrations and mixtures of those pharmaceuticals in the effluents of 2 WWTPs that receive discharge from PFFs with pharmaceutical concentrations from another WWTP that does not receive PFF discharge (data collected between from 2004 to 2009), and (3) describes the persistence of these 7 pharmaceuticals in streamwater samples collected downstream from three selected WWTPs from 2004 to 2009. The research detailed in this report was undertaken in cooperation with the U.S. Geological Survey (USGS) and the New York State Department of Environmental Conservation.

Purpose and Scope

This report documents the data and presents supporting information associated with the study by Phillips and others (2010). This report includes

- a description of the sampling network used in the study;
- available information on the pharmaceuticals formulated at the two PFFs that discharge to two WWTPs in New York State included in the study;
- a description of the analytical methods used in the study, including chemicals analyzed for, sample preparation, qualitative and tentative identification of analytes, quantitation of analytes, and method performance information; and
- environmental data generated by the study, including quality-assurance data; chemical data from WWTPs, streams and reservoirs; and flow data associated with selected samples from WWTPs and streamwater samples.

Concentrations of seven selected pharmaceutical compounds in streamwater, reservoir water, and effluent from WWTPs in New York State are presented in tables and illustrations. Concentrations of those pharmaceuticals for 23 WWTPs across the United States also are presented in tables and illustrations.

Sampling Network

A comprehensive listing of all sites sampled in this study is provided in table 1. Samples were collected from 26 WWTPs, including 23 WWTPs sampled once as part of a national survey and three WWTPs located in New York State that were sampled multiple times. Twenty-three WWTPs in 12 states across the United States were sampled once during 2006-09 (four as 24-hour flow composites and 19 as grab samples) as part of a national survey. More than half of the 23 WWTPs in the national survey receive discharge from hospitals.

Three WWTPs in New York State (sites NY1, NY2, and NY3) were sampled 35 to 38 times during 2004-09 (table 2). Approximately 20 percent of the total wastewater inflow to WWTPs NY2 and NY3 is discharge from a PFF; WWTP NY2 also receives discharge from a hospital. WWTP NY1 does not receive hospital or PFF discharge. More than 30 streamwater samples were collected within a few km (kilometers) downstream from the outfall of WWTPs NY1, NY2, and NY3 using standard width- and depth-integrating techniques. The distance downstream from the WWTP discharge points and the amount of dilution in terms of the effluent as a percent of streamflow for the downstream sites are given in table 3. No tributaries enter the streams between the effluent discharge points and the downstream sampling locations.

Site codes, USGS site numbers, and the site names for all sites sampled as part of this study are included in table 4. In addition to the sites discussed in the preceding paragraphs, sites located upstream from the three NY WWTPs were sampled for streamwater (table 4). No tributaries enter the stream between the sampling site on the stream above the WWTP and the effluent discharge sampling site for sites NY1 and NY2. At the NY3 site, a small tributary enters the stream between the upstream main-stem sampling location and the NY3 effluent discharge. Because two streams join just before the NY3 effluent discharge point, both of these streams were sampled to represent pharmaceutical concentrations in streamwater upstream from the NY3 effluent discharge point. Between 1 and 16 samples were collected from 10 reservoirs in New York State (table 4) during 2006-09. Many of these samples (16) were collected from RES01, a drinking water reservoir 30 km downstream of site NY2. Additional streamwater samples were collected downstream from or near the NY2 WWTP effluent discharge point to characterize pharmaceutical concentrations in this setting (table 4). Finally, three sites are included in table 4 that correspond to additional sites with data from blank samples.

Table 1. Descriptions of 23 wastewater-treatment plants sampled once during 2006-09 in a national survey of wastewater-treatment-plant effluent and three wastewater-treatment plants in New York State sampled multiple times during 2004-09.

[All sites except IA2, NY1, and NY4 use activated sludge for biologic treatment; site NY4 uses rotating biologic contactor; sites IA2 and NY1 use trickling filter. Samples from sites CA1, MD1, NY1, NY2, NY3, and VT1 were collected as 24 hour flow-weighed composites. A dash (-) in the column for pharmaceutical source indicates neither a hospital nor a pharmaceutical manufacturer discharges to the site. m^3/s, cubic meters per second]

Site code	Location	Population served	Pharmaceutical source: hospital (H) or pharmaceutical manufacturer (P)	Effluent discharge rate (m^3/s)
National survey				
AZ1	Arizona-1	500,000	H	1.0
AZ2	Arizona-2	1,000,000	H	1.4
CA1	California	4,000,000	H	20
CO1	Colorado	110,000	H	1.1
FL1	Florida	1,250,000	H	8.8
IA1	Iowa-1	25,000	H	0.22
IA2	Iowa-2	42,000	-	0.38
MD1	Maryland	1,300,000	H	7.9
MT1	Montana-1	30,000	H	0.12
NV1	Nevada	300,000	H	1.3
NY4	New York-4	800	-	0.0033
NY5	New York-5	200	-	0.0027
NY6	New York-6	1,000	-	0.013
NY7	New York-7	1,350	-	0.0088
NY8	New York-8	3,500	-	0.051
NY9	New York-9	800	H	0.011
TX1	Texas-1	1,200,000	H	3.2
TX2	Texas-2	1,400	-	0.013
TX3	Texas-3	37,000	H	3.3
VT1	Vermont-1	31,000	-	0.20
VT2	Vermont-2	7,000	H	0.044
WI1	Wisconsin-1	1,100,000	H	4.40
WI2	Wisconsin-2	330,000	H	1.80
New York sites sampled multiple times				
NY1	New York-1	10,000	-	0.061
NY2	New York-2	3,000	H,P	0.031
NY3	New York-3	400	P	0.0031

Table 2. Number of effluent samples collected from wastewater treatment plants and streamwater samples collected at sites NY1, NY2, and NY3 in New York State during 2004-09, and types of treatment provided by each wastewater treatment plant.

Site	Number of effluent samples	Number of downstream samples	Secondary biological treatment	Tertiary treatment	Disinfection
NY1	36	35	Trickling Filter	Sand filtration	Chlorination/dechlorination
NY2	35	36	Two-Stage activated sludge	Sand filtration	Chlorination/dechlorination
NY3	38	36	Extended aeration activated sludge	Sand/anthracite micro-filtration	Ultraviolet

Table 3. Distance downstream and effluent dilution at three stream sampling sites in New York State, 2004-09.

[km, kilometers; L/s, liters per second]

Site	Distance downstream (km)	Median effluent discharge (L/s)	Median streamflow (L/s)	Median percent of streamflow from effluent
NY1	0.01	53	330	15
NY2	1.2	30	120	24
NY3	6.1	2.8	1,500	0.17

Table 4. Sites sampled across the United States during 2004-09 (Excel format).

Information on Pharmaceuticals Formulated at PFFs

Publically available information on pharmaceuticals formulated at the PMFs is limited. Such information can be useful for designing studies that characterize the potential pharmaceutical source loadings to the environment from a PMF. Information provided in this report on pharmaceuticals formulated at PFFs that discharge to WWTPs NY2 and NY3 is based on the following sources:

(1) Direct USFDA (Food and Drug Administration) identification of selected pharmaceuticals formulated at these sites (Suzanne Fitzpatrick, Food and Drug Administration, written commun., 2009),

(2) A New York State report indicating use of two pharmaceuticals at the PFF discharging to NY3 (New York State Department of Environmental Conservation, 2009),

(3) A web site operated by The U.S. National Institutes of Health (NIH) that provides labels for select pharmaceuticals, identifying the company marketing the pharmaceutical or the company manufacturing the pharmaceutical (Daily Med, 2009), and

(4) Manufacturers' web sites that list the pharmaceuticals marketed by the owners of the PFFs (Covidien, 2009; Watson Pharmaceuticals, 2009).

Method Description

The method of analysis of the selected pharmaceuticals is based on a previously developed method for the determination of 61 compounds typically found in domestic and industrial wastewater (Zaugg and others, 2002). The changes to the existing method included identification and quantitation of seven additional analytes but did not include any change to extraction or other procedures. A brief explanation of the method and approach to adding analytes is provided here; a detailed description of the overall method is available in Zaugg and others (2002).

The seven additional pharmaceuticals were selected primarily because full-scan gas chromatography/mass spectrometry analysis of samples from sites NY1, NY2, and NY3 prior to this study indicated that these pharmaceuticals were commonly present as tentatively identified compounds in samples analyzed for organic waste indicator compounds. Several of these pharmaceuticals are among the most commonly prescribed medications in the United States (Lamb, 2009), yet limited environmental occurrence data are available for these pharmaceuticals in the United States. All seven target pharmaceuticals are listed in table 5; all but carisoprodol were analyzed for in samples collected during this study (2004-09), whereas carisoprodol was analyzed for in all samples collected after March 2006.

Table 5. List of seven target pharmaceuticals with chemical properties and method detection limit.
[CASRN, CAS Registry Number®; Kow, octanol-water partition coefficient; mg/L, milligram per liter; μg/L, microgram per liter]

Analyte	CASRN[a]	Compound class	Log Kow[b]	Water solubility (mg/L)[b]	Method detection limit[c] (μg/L)
Butalbital	77-26-9	Barbiturate	1.87	1,700	0.014
Carisoprodol	78-44-4	Muscle relaxant	2.36	300	0.021
Diazepam	439-14-5	Benzodiazepine tranquilizer	2.82	50.0	0.012
Metaxalone	1665-48-1	Muscle relaxant	2.60	90.7	0.011
Methadone	76-99-3	Opioid	3.93	48.5	0.044
Oxycodone	76-42-6	Opioid	0.66	4,160	0.076
Phendimetrazine	634-03-7	Amphetamine	1.70	17,300	0.021

[a] This report contains CAS Registry Numbers®, which is a Registered Trademark of the American Chemical Society. CAS recommends the verification of the CASRNs through CAS Client Services[SM].

[b] Chemical properties from online database http://www.syrres.com/esc/physdemo htm (accessed January 2008).

[c] Method detection limits were determined from 10 reagent water samples fortified at 0.05 μg/L and 7 reagent water samples fortified at 0.20 μg/L.

Sample Preparation, Apparatus, Instrumentation, and Standards

One-liter samples were filtered through 0.7 μm (micrometer) glass-fiber filters prior to solid-phase extraction (SPE). After filtration, three surrogate compounds (table 6) were added to each environmental and (or) quality-control sample to monitor sample-specific method performance. Laboratory reagent blank and reagent set spike samples were prepared with each set of as many as 10 environmental samples. Samples were extracted by vacuum filtration through 500-mg (milligram) OASIS-HLB-SPE cartridges (Waters Inc., catalog number 186000115) using a custom extraction manifold; the desired extraction flow-rate range was 25 to 50 mL/min (milliliters per minute). (The use of trade, firm, or brand names in this paper is for identification purposes only and does not constitute endorsement by the USGS.) SPE Cartridges were eluted with dichloromethane:diethyl ether, 80:20 volume per volume. Sample extracts were evaporated to 0.4 mL, placed in a 1.5-mL autosampler vial. Internal standards were added, and the sample was held at -4° C (degrees Celsius) until instrumental analysis was performed. Sample extracts were analyzed using capillary gas chromatography/mass spectrometry (GC/MS, Agilent Technologies model 6890 GC and model 5973 MS) and operated under full scan conditions and using electron impact ionization at 70 eV (electron volts).

Table 6. Retention time, quantitation ion, and confirmation ions for target analytes, surrogate compounds, and internal standard reference compounds.

[min, minutes; m/z, mass-to-charge ratio; -- no data]

Analyte	Retention time (min)	Quantitation ion (m/z)	Confirmation ion (m/z)	Confirmation ion (m/z)
Analytes				
Butalbital	30.96	168	167	181
Carisoprodol	33.53	245	158	184
Diazepam	38.70	256	283	221
Metaxalone	36.32	122	221	107
Methadone	36.13	294	72	165
Oxycodone	39.53	315	258	230
Phendimetrazine	27.74	191	51	85
Surrogates				
Caffeine-d_9	33.07	203	115	--
Decafluorobiphenyl	19.59	334	265	--
Fluoranthene-d_{10}	36.31	212	106	--
Internal Standards				
Acenaphthene-d_{10}	28.64	164	162	160
Chrysene-d_{12}	38.79	240	--	--
Perylene-d_{12}	41.97	264	132	--
Phenanthrene-d_{10}	32.63	188	--	--

The GC conditions were:
- ☐ Column: HP Ultra II (5 percent phenylmethyl silicone), 30 m (meter) x 0.25 mm (millimeter), 0.50 μm film thickness;
- ☐ Carrier gas: ultra high purity helium with a linear-flow velocity of 32 cm/s (centimeter per second);
- ☐ Injection port temperature: 290° C; 1 μL (microliter) volume;
- ☐ Split vent open 0.7 min;
- ☐ GC oven temperature program: initial temperature, 40° C, then ramp rate 4° C/min to 100° C, then 8° C/min to 350° C, hold time 2 min at 350° C.

The mass spectrometer conditions were:
- ☐ Ionization energy: 70 eV,
- ☐ Operation: Full-scan from 50 to 450 atomic mass units at 1 scan/sec.
- ☐ Temperatures: source 230° C, GC/MS interface 290° C.

Metaxalone and phendimetrazine standards were obtained from Toronto Research Chemicals. All the remaining standards were obtained from Fisher Scientific. Purity for all compounds was 99 percent or better.

Qualitative and Tentative Identification of Analytes

Detection of a target analyte was reported only if it met qualitative GC/MS criteria (retention time, comparison to reference standard mass spectra including ion-abundance ratios; see table 6). This qualitative criteria required that (1) GC retention time was within ±0.05 minute of that of the authentic standard, and (2) the mass spectral quantitation ion and two confirmation ion abundance ratios were within ±20 percent of the standard values.

Besides the seven target analytes, additional pharmaceuticals were subsequently identified qualitatively in at least two samples collected during 2008-09. Authentic standards were obtained for comparison; the qualitative criteria include confirmation of GC retention time and mass spectral abundance. Ions used for qualification for these additional pharmaceuticals are listed in table 7.

Tentatively identified compounds (TIC) were observed and are reported in this paper according to guidelines indicated in the U.S. Geological Survey Office of Water Quality Technical Memorandum 90.11 (Rickert, 1990). TICs were identified by comparing mass spectra collected from environmental samples to reference mass spectra in the National Institute of Standards and Technology NIST05a mass spectral reference library. The NIST05a library is a reference MS (mass spectrometry) spectral library of pure compounds collected under full scan mode under 70 eV electron-impact ionization conditions. A computer comparison algorithm, proprietary to the MS software used, was applied to each TIC spectra to identify the best fit candidate library spectra, followed by visual comparison of the reference and TIC. TICs suspected of being derived from pharmaceuticals that had a probability match factor of 70 or greater and which were visually confirmed by the analyst were reported.

Table 7. Measured retention time, quantitation ion, and confirmation ions for qualitatively identified compounds.

[min, minutes; m/z, mass-to-charge ratio]

Analyte	Retention time (min)	Quantitation ion (m/z)	Confirmation ion (m/z)	Confirmation ion (m/z)
2-Ethyl-2-phenylmalonamide	33.97	163	148	120
Acetaminophen	31.03	109	151	80
Bupropion	29.71	100	139	224
Chlorpheniramine	35.05	203	205	167
Codeine	38.40	299	229	162
Dihydrocodeine	38.42	301	284	286
Diltiazem	42.40	58	71	150
Fluoxetine	33.55	309	148	104
Hydrocodone	38.90	299	242	214
Meperidine	32.18	71	247	246
Meprobamate	32.54	83	144	114
Methylphenidate	32.00	84	91	150
Methocarbamol	35.18	118	109	124
o-Desmethyltramadol	35.20	58	121	249
Phenobarbital	34.67	204	232	117
Primidone	37.10	190	146	117
Temazepam	39.89	271	300	256
Tramadol	34.51	58	263	135
Verapamil	43.84	303	151	58

Quantitation of Analytes

Target analytes that met the qualitative identification criteria were quantified using the injection internal standard method using a 5 to 8 point calibration curve (Zaugg and others, 2002).

Quantifying High Concentrations

The method used in this study was initially designed to quantify environmental concentrations of the target analytes in the general range of 10 µg/L and less. The initial maximum calibration point for most compounds was 40 µg/L, with the exception of diazepam (4 µg/L), and metaxalone (400 µg/L).

Because concentrations exceeding the uppermost value on the calibration curve were consistently detected in effluents from two WWTPs (NY2 and NY3), calibration curves were extended during the course of the study. For samples collected after March 2009, calibration curves were extended to allow for quantitation over a broader range of concentrations, and maximum calibration points were extended to 400 µg/L for all compounds except metaxalone, which was extended to 4,000 µg/L. Concentrations exceeding the calibration curve were censored and reported as greater than (>) the concentration of the maximum calibration point.

For selected samples collected before the higher calibration standards were used, concentrations were quantified above the maximum calibration point using the higher calibration curves and (or) by (1) diluting samples, (2) extracting lesser amounts of sample, or (3) analysis of frozen archived samples. Overall, much of the data from site NY3 effluent samples were affected by the calibration curve dynamic range limitation with from 20 percent to 60 percent of samples right-censored for butalbital, metaxalone, methadone, and oxycodone. A few samples (less than 20 percent) were right-censored at 40 µg/L for butalbital and carisoprodol in samples collected from NY2 effluent.

Quantifying Low Concentrations

For samples collected before August 1, 2007, minimum calibration points were 0.4 µg/L for all analytes except diazepam (0.04 µg/L) and metaxalone (4 µg/L). After this time, the minimum calibration point was extended to 0.04 µg/L for most analytes, to 0.004 µg/L for diazepam, and to 0.4 µg/L for metaxalone. Some low-level concentrations are reported that are greater than the method detection limit (MDL) but less than the lowest point on the calibration curve, particularly for samples collected before August 2007. These estimated values are identified as such herein and were generally within 50 percent of the lowest point on the calibration curve.

Method Performance

This section details the method performance tests that were undertaken to insure that the data generated by the modified analytical method were of high quality. The assessments of method performance include a variety of spikes, a method detection limit study, a study to estimate precision, and a holding time study. The measures of method performance discussed below reflect (1) method performance results collected over the entire period when environmental samples were analyzed and (2) specific method performance evaluations made after the range of concentrations likely to occur was better understood.

Spikes

A variety of spike experiments were performed to characterize method performance. Reagent set spike samples were reagent water samples fortified with known amounts of the eight pharmaceuticals and processed with a set of environmental samples. The final fortification concentration reflects the sensitivity of each compound in the analysis. Individual reagent set spike samples were used to evaluate set-specific method performance in the absence of sample matrix components. The individual reagent set spike results can be used to assess overall method bias and precision by aggregating individual reagent set spike samples and calculating mean recoveries and relative standard deviations (RSDs). Reagent set spike recoveries reflect method performance in the absence of coextracted sample matrix components. In order to better assess these contrasting matrix effects on the seven pharmaceuticals in this study, replicate samples from three different wastewater sources and a streamwater sample collected upstream from one of these wastewater discharge points were fortified with all or a select group of these pharmaceuticals, and recoveries were determined after correction for ambient compound concentrations from analysis of two or more unspiked replicates.

Reagent Set Spikes

Reagent set spike data were divided into two periods corresponding to different spiking concentrations. Data on reagent set spike samples analyzed before 2009 are given in table 8, and those for 2009 are given in table 9. Spike concentrations were higher for the reagent set spikes analyzed before 2009; spike concentrations were decreased for analyses in 2009 to better correspond to concentrations typically present in samples. Results of analyses of reagent set spike recoveries over the duration of the study indicated no temporal trends, further indicating method performance was stable over the course of the study. The differences between pre-2009 and 2009 reagent set spike recoveries and RSDs are likely due to the difference in spiking levels and to a lesser extent the difference in the number of spikes between the two periods.

Table 8. Mean recovery and relative standard deviation of pharmaceuticals from reagent set spike samples analyzed before 2009.
[RSD, relative standard deviation].

Analyte	Number of spikes	Fortification concentration, in micrograms per liter	Mean percent recovery	Percent RSD
Butalbital	54	8	82	18
Carisoprodol	54	8	113	21
Diazepam	54	0.8	96	23
Metaxalone	54	80	102	14
Methadone	54	8	70	28
Oxycodone	54	8	72	34
Phendimetrazine	54	8	86	22

Table 9. Mean recovery and relative standard deviation of pharmaceuticals from reagent set spike samples for 2009.
[RSD, relative standard deviation]

Analyte	Number of spikes	Fortification concentration, in micrograms per liter	Mean percent recovery	Percent RSD
Butalbital	24	0.2	124	22
Carisoprodol	24	0.2	140	27
Diazepam	24	0.2	111	17
Metaxalone	24	0.2	118	23
Methadone	24	0.2	66	25
Oxycodone	15	0.2	105	46
Phendimetrazine	19	0.2	83	21

Mean reagent set spike recoveries for both sets of reagent set spike data range from 66 percent to 140 percent, and RSDs are generally less than 30 percent. The only mean reagent set spike outside the 60 percent to 130 percent range is the low-concentration carisoprodol spike (140 percent). Only two RSDs are greater than 30 percent: RSDs for the oxycodone low-concentration and high-concentration spikes are 34 and 46 percent, respectively.

Matrix Spikes

The four matrix spike samples include: (1) an NY3 effluent spiked at high concentrations (5-4,000 µg/L), (2) an NY1 effluent sample spiked at moderate (0.8-80 µg/L) concentrations, (3) an NY4 effluent sample spiked at low (0.2 µg/L) concentrations, and (4) a streamwater sample collected upstream from the NY1 WWTP discharge point (hereafter referred to as the NY1 upstream sample) spiked at low–moderate concentrations (0.08-8 µg/L). The number of replicate samples spiked range from 5 to 13 for each matrix spike. These matrices included various wastewaters with a wide range of expected pharmaceutical concentrations and a streamwater with no effluent discharge.

NY3 Effluent Matrix Spikes

A single composite sample of NY3 effluent collected in May 2009 was divided into six replicate 1-L (liter) samples, and fortified with six of the seven analytes (all but diazepam) at high concentrations (5 to 4,000 µg/L) to assess method performance for very high analyte concentrations in wastewater-enriched environmental samples. These samples were extracted and analyzed in a single analytical set. Any ambient environmental contributions of analytes to the matrix spike replicates were corrected for by duplicate analysis of unspiked samples. Results for the six effluent samples spiked with analytes are listed in table 10. For the six analytes with available data, mean recoveries and RSDs of analytes fortified with high concentrations in samples of NY3 effluent (table 10) are similar to recoveries and RSDs observed in reagent set spikes (tables 8, 9). All analytes for the NY3 effluent spiked samples have recoveries of 60 percent to 130 percent, and RSDs were all less than 30 percent.

Table 10. Mean spike recoveries and percent relative standard deviations for six replicate matrix spikes of effluent from wastewater treatment plant NY3 in New York State, fortified over a range of high concentrations for six analytes.

[RSD, relative standard deviation; Diazepam was not spiked in these samples so that data for this analyte is not available; µg/L, micrograms per liter]

Analyte	Fortification concentration, in micrograms per liter	Mean percent recovery	Percent RSD
Butalbital	12 - 402	87	2.8
Carisoprodol	20 - 800	94	13
Metaxalone	104 - 4,000	77	11
Methadone	92 - 871	63	12
Oxycodone	24 - 804	70	11
Phendimetrazine	22 - 802	70	16

NY1 Effluent Matrix Spikes

A single composite sample of NY1 effluent collected in March 2007 was divided into five replicate 1-L samples and fortified with the analytes at moderate (0.8 to 80 µg/L) concentrations to assess method performance for moderate analyte concentrations in wastewater-enriched environmental samples. These samples were extracted and analyzed in a single analytical set. Any ambient environmental contributions of analytes to the matrix spike replicates were corrected for by duplicate analysis of unspiked samples. Results for the five effluent samples spiked with seven analytes are listed in table 11.

Table 11. Mean spike recoveries and percent relative standard deviations for five replicate matrix spikes of effluent from wastewater-treatment plant NY1 in New York State, fortified at moderate concentrations for seven analytes.

[RSD, relative standard deviation]

Analyte	Fortification concentration, in micrograms per liter	Mean percent recovery	Percent RSD
Butalbital	8	95	7.2
Carisoprodol	8	104	6.1
Diazepam	0.8	94	4.6
Metaxalone	80	96	5.9
Methadone	8	59	27
Oxycodone	8	94	7.4
Phendimetrazine	8	66	26

Mean recoveries and RSDs of analytes fortified with moderate concentrations in samples of NY1 effluent (table 11) are similar to recoveries and RSDs observed for reagent set spikes (tables 8, 9) and those for the NY3 effluent spike samples (table 10). All but one of the mean recoveries are within the 60 percent to 130 percent range, and all RSDs were less than 30 percent. The only recovery outside the 60 percent to 130 percent range is methadone (59 percent; table 11). As was the case for NY3 effluent spikes, many of these analytes have RSDs that are lower in these matrix spikes than in reagent set spikes. This is attributed to the analysis of these samples in a single set; the reagent set spikes were analyzed in multiple sets over several years.

NY4 Effluent Matrix Spikes

A single composite sample of NY4 effluent collected in May 2009 was divided into 13 replicate 1-L samples and fortified with the analytes at low (0.2 µg/L) concentrations to assess method performance for low analyte concentrations in wastewater-enriched environmental samples. The NY4 effluent sample was spiked so that an effluent sample would be included in spiking experiments from the set of 23 WWTP effluent samples in the national survey. Any ambient environmental contributions of analytes to the matrix spike replicates were corrected for by triplicate analysis of unspiked samples. These 13 replicate samples were extracted in 5 different extraction sets and then analyzed in a single analytical set.

Results for the spiked analytes are listed in Table 12. These samples were also used for a holding time study (see below). Data for all the analytes but phendimetrazine are available; the data for phendimetrazine from the NY4 effluent spike holding time experiment are not included because there was a significant decrease in the concentration for this analyte over the 15 day holding time experiment. Thus, with the exception of phendimetrazine, the aggregated results could also be used as a matrix spike recovery experiment.

Five of the six analytes with available data for NY4 Effluent spikes have mean percent recoveries within the 60 percent to 130 percent range, and all but one of the RSDs are less than 30 percent. Recoveries for oxycodone (170 percent) are higher than the other analyte recoveries in this spike, but the RSD is low (8.8 percent). Only the methadone RSD exceeds 30 percent (31 percent). For most analytes, the recoveries were higher and RSDs are similar to those for reagent set spikes (tables 8, 9) and other effluent matrix spikes (tables 10, 11). The high mean recovery for oxycodone in this spike may reflect the low spiking level used in this experiment.

Table 12. Mean spike recoveries and percent relative standard deviations for 13 replicate matrix spikes of effluent from wastewater-treatment plant NY4 in New York State, fortified at low concentrations for six analytes.

[RSD, relative standard deviation]

Analyte	Fortification concentration, in micrograms per liter	Mean percent recovery	Percent RSD
Butalbital	0.2	120	10
Carisoprodol	0.2	99	5.1
Diazepam	0.2	110	6.5
Metaxalone	0.2	120	5.1
Methadone	0.2	91	31
Oxycodone	0.2	170	8.8

NY1 Upstream Matrix Spikes

A single composite sample of streamwater collected upstream from NY1 in March 2007 was divided into five replicate 1-L samples, and fortified with target analytes at low (0.08-8 μg/L) concentrations to assess method performance for low analyte concentrations in environmental waters with negligible wastewater content. These samples were extracted and analyzed in a single analytical set. Any ambient environmental contributions of analytes to the matrix spike replicates were corrected for by duplicate analysis of unspiked samples. Results for the seven samples spiked with analytes are listed in table 13.

Table 13. Mean spike recoveries and percent relative standard deviations for five replicate matrix spikes of streamwater collected upstream of the NY1 effluent discharge in New York State, fortified at low concentrations for seven analytes.

[RSD, relative standard deviation]

Analyte	Fortification concentration, in micrograms per liter	Mean percent recovery	Percent RSD
Butalbital	0.8	93	14
Carisoprodol	0.8	97	13
Diazepam	0.08	97	8.2
Metaxalone	8	87	8.5
Methadone	0.8	32	48
Oxycodone	0.8	57	36
Phendimetrazine	0.8	57	23

Four analytes (butalbital, carisoprodol, diazepam, and metaxalone) have mean recoveries of 60 percent to 130 percent, and five have RSDs less than 30 percent in the NY1 upstream spike. Two pharmaceuticals (oxycodone and phendimetrazine) have recoveries of 57 percent and RSDs of 36 percent and 23 percent, respectively. Methadone has a low recovery (32 percent) and high RSD (48 percent) for this spike. These mean recoveries and RSDs are somewhat lower for some analytes than the recoveries and RSDs observed for the reagent set spikes (tables 8, 9) and for the matrix spike samples of effluent (tables 10–12) for some analytes.

Summary of Reagent Set and Matrix Spikes

Data from the different spike experiments (two reagent set spike experiments with low and medium analyte concentrations, three effluent spike experiments with low, medium and high concentrations, and a stream spike experiment with medium concentrations) show that median mean recoveries for all spikes are 94 percent, and median RSDs are 15 percent. For the 14 reagent set spikes, only the mean recovery for the low concentration (0.2 µg/L) carisoprodol spike (140 percent; table 9) lies outside the 60 percent to 130 percent range, and only the two oxycodone spikes have RSDs greater than 30 percent (low level at 46 percent and high level at 34 percent). Of the 19 effluent spikes, two mean recoveries — methadone for the moderate concentration NY1 effluent spike (59 percent; table 11) and oxycodone for the low-level NY4 effluent spike (170 percent; table 12) have mean recoveries outside the 60 percent to 130 percent range. Only one of the 19 effluent spikes, the low concentration methadone NY4 effluent, has an RSD greater than 30 percent (31 percent).

The effluent spiking results show that the seven analytes have low bias and variability for the effluent matrix. Although the low-level reagent spikes indicate that carisoprodol may have a positive bias for low concentrations, the recoveries for the other reagent spikes and effluent samples spiked with carisoprodol range from 99 percent to 104 percent, indicating no bias. Results of the methadone effluent spike with middle range (8 µg/L) concentrations indicate a slight low bias (mean recovery of 59 percent), yet the results for the other two methadone effluent spikes with low (0.2 µg/L) and high (≥90 µg/L) range concentrations (63 percent and 91 percent, respectively) show no bias. The results indicate a positive bias for oxycodone at low concentrations (0.2 µg/L), yet the two other oxycodone effluent spikes for moderate (8 µg/L) and high (≥24 µg/L) concentrations have mean recoveries of 94 percent and 70 percent, respectively. The high RSDs for reagent set spikes indicate that oxycodone concentrations may be more variable than those of other pharmaceuticals in this study; however the three effluent spikes for oxycodone all have RSDs less than 30 percent.

The streamwater spike recoveries for butalbital, carisoprodol, diazepam and metaxalone range from 60 percent to 130 percent, with RSDs less than 30 percent, indicating low bias and variability. Because of the low (32 percent) and variable (RSD of 48 percent) recovery for methadone stream-water spikes, stream-water data for methadone are reported only qualitatively (as percent detection). The low recoveries for streamwater oxycodone and phendimetrazine spikes (both 57 percent) indicate that the concentrations of these two analytes in streamwater may be biased low. In addition, the RSD for the oxycodone spike in streamwater is 36 percent, indicating a higher variability for concentrations in streamwater of this pharmaceutical than for the others.

Method Detection Limit

The determination of MDLs for each pharmaceutical was conducted according to the procedures of the U.S. Environmental Protection Agency (2005), and MDLs are presented in table 14. MDLs were calculated using the following equation.

$$MDL = S \times T(n\text{-}1, 1\text{-}alpha\text{=}0.99) \ (1),$$

where

S is standard deviation of replicate analysis, in micrograms per liter, at the lowest spike concentration;

n is number of replicate analyses;

and

T(n-1, 1-alpha=0.99) is Student's t-value for the 99 percent confidence level with n-1 degrees of freedom.

The MDLs were determined using a low-level reagent spike study that employed multiple experiments in order to ensure that the lowest appropriate spiking level was used to calculate each individual MDL. These experiments resulted in data that provide reagent set spike recoveries near the detection limit as well as MDLs, which are discussed together in this section. Two fortification concentrations were used. Ten reagent water samples were fortified at 0.05 µg/L for each compound, extracted, and analyzed. These samples were analyzed in the same analytical set. Seven reagent water samples were fortified at 0.2 µg/L for each analyte, extracted, and analyzed. These samples also served as set spikes, and were prepared and analyzed in different analytical sets. Details on the mean recoveries, percent RSDs, and calculated MDLs at both fortification concentrations are shown in table 14.

Table 14. Mean recoveries, percent relative standard deviations, and method detection limits calculated from reagent water samples fortified at 0.05 µg/L and 0.2 µg/L.

[RSD, relative standard deviation in percent; MDL, method detection limit; ND, not detected; --, data not calculated; µg/L micrograms per liter; n, number of replicates. Method detection limits values in **bold** correspond to those used as final method detection limits.]

Analyte	0.05 µg/L fortification (n=10)			0.20 µg/L fortification (n=7)		
	Mean percent recovery	Percent RSD	MDL, in µg/L	Mean percent recovery	Percent RSD	MDL, in µg/L
Butalbital	112	9	**0.014**	110	5.6	0.036
Carisoprodol	97	15	**0.021**	100	5.9	0.035
Diazepam	125	7	**0.012**	110	5.4	0.034
Metaxalone	99	8	**0.011**	110	4.4	0.029
Methadone	57	13	--	74	10	**0.044**
Oxycodone	ND	--	--	94	14	**0.076**
Phendimetrazine	52	28	**0.021**	69	24	0.098

Five of the seven analytes (butalbital, carisoprodol, diazepam, metaxalone, and phendimetrazine) were reliably detected in the 0.05 µg/L fortification samples, and the MDLs at this fortification were used as MDLs in the study (table 14). The remaining two analytes (methadone and oxycodone) were detectable at 0.20 µg/L (table 14). Although a mean recovery could be calculated for methadone in the 0.05-µg/L fortification level, methadone was detected in only 7 of the 10 samples fortified at 0.05 µg/L, so the results of the 0.20-µg/L fortification level were used for methadone. Mean recoveries and RSDs of the five analytes reliably detected at the 0.05-μg/L fortification level are comparable to the mean recoveries and RSDs at the 0.2 μg/L fortification and in the range typical for reagent set spikes (see tables 8, 9). All mean recoveries and RSDs at the 0.2-μg/L fortification level are comparable to mean recoveries and RSDs in the reagent set spike results (tables 8, 9). The spiking concentrations used for MDL determinations were appropriate, because the spiking levels are within 1 to 5 times the MDLs.

Estimation of Precision

In order to better understand precision in the analysis of environmental samples, 18 replicates of a homogeneous sample of NY3 effluent were analyzed, and method precision was calculated. The replicates were prepared for analysis in five different preparation sets, but instrumental analysis was conducted as a single set. These replicates also were used for a holding time study (see below), and thus, the calculated precision better incorporates sources of variation associated with different preparation sets. The results of this experiment are shown in table 15. Because these data represent the environmental concentrations in NY3 effluent at the time of sample collection, all analytes were not present. Most analytes (5 of 7) were detected in the sample of NY3 effluent, allowing for the assessment of precision for most of the analytes included in the study; the RSDs for these five compounds range from 5.1 percent to 21 percent. This precision is comparable to other estimates of precision for environmental samples made for pharmaceuticals and wastewater indicator compounds included in previous studies (Glassmeyer and others, 2005).

Table 15. Mean concentrations and percent relative standard deviations calculated for ambient pharmaceuticals in 18 replicate 1-liter sample aliquots from effluent collected at site NY3, New York State, 2009.

[RSD, relative standard deviation, in percent.]

Analyte	Mean concentration, in micrograms per liter	Percent RSD
Butalbital	1.6	5.2
Metaxalone	4.23	5.1
Methadone	71.7	11
Oxycodone	3.7	21
Phendimetrazine	1.79	6.4

Holding Time Study

The method of analysis used in this study was based on a recommended holding time (Zaugg and others, 2002) of up to 14 days for filtered water samples. Since these samples were comprised of treated wastewater, however, separate holding time studies were conducted in order to assess whether the maximum recommended 14-day holding time would introduce systematic low bias into the results as a result of potential degradation of the seven pharmaceuticals of interest. Two studies were conducted using multiple aliquots of samples collected at the NY3 and NY4 WWTP sites. The NY4 sample aliquots were fortified with the seven analytes and these aliquots analyzed over a 14-day period. The NY3 replicate sample aliquots were not fortified and were also analyzed over a 14-day period. Two experiments were conducted to include an assessment of long holding times for a range of wastewater-treatment matrices, as the NY3 effluent was from an activated sludge wastewater plant, and the NY4 effluent was from a rotating biologic contactor wastewater plant. These data were useful for ensuring that holding time information was available for all seven analytes included in the study, and for indicating whether results would be different for unfortified samples (NY3) and fortified samples (NY4).

Eighteen NY3 replicate effluent samples were analyzed to determine compound degradation in sample matrix with respect to time. None of these samples were fortified, because they contained high ambient environmental concentrations of most (five) of the seven analytes. Three samples were extracted within 24 hours of sampling. Three samples were extracted 3 days from collection, then 3 more samples were extracted on days 5, 7, 11, and 15. Linear regression analysis of concentration versus hold time was performed to calculate a degradation rate. This rate was used to determine the percentage of analyte lost to degradation in 15 days. The results of the holding time study for these unfortified samples are shown in table 16.

Table 16. Percent change in concentration for pharmaceuticals in unfortified wastewater treatment plant samples from NY3, New York State, and fortified effluent samples from NY4 after 15 days.
[Negative results indicate a decrease, and positive results indicate an increase in concentration; ND, no data]

Analyte	Percent change in concentration in unfortified NY3 effluent	Percent change in concentration in fortified NY4 effluent
Butalbital	-1.7	1.3
Carisoprodol	ND	-7.3
Diazepam	ND	-3.6
Metaxalone	-1.0	-3.9
Methadone	0.3	-6.9
Oxycodone	-7.3	-5.8
Phendimetrazine	1.2	-45

Sixteen NY4 replicate effluent samples were studied to determine compound degradation in sample matrix with respect to time. Thirteen 1-L replicate samples were fortified in the field at 0.2 μg/L for all seven target pharmaceuticals at the time of collection. Three additional samples were collected but not spiked. The three unspiked samples and three spiked samples were extracted within 24 hours of sampling. Three samples were extracted three days from collection and three more seven days from collection. Two samples were extracted 11 days from collection and two more were extracted 15 days from collection. Linear regression analysis of concentration versus hold time was performed to determine a degradation rate for each pharmaceutical. This rate was used to determine the percent of analyte lost to degradation in 15 days. The rates for all analytes are shown in table 16.

For both the NY3 and NY4 holding time experiments, four pharmaceuticals (butalbital, methadone, oxycodone, and metaxalone) had small (less than 8 percent) changes in concentrations over the 15 days (table 16). Two other pharmaceuticals, detected only in the NY4 effluent (carisoprodol and diazepam) had small (less than 8 percent) decreases in concentrations after 15 days (table 16). Phendimetrazine had slight increases (1.2 percent) in concentrations in NY3 effluent samples but large (45 percent) decreases in concentrations in NY4 effluent spike at

15 days. The lower concentrations of phendimetrazine in the NY4 effluent spike indicate that this sample matrix may result in degradation of these analytes in samples over 15 days. Overall, for most of the target pharmaceuticals, there was little indication of positive or negative bias over 15 days, but some effluent matrices could result in a decrease in concentrations for phendimetrazine over a 15-day holding time. The median holding time for the environmental samples included in the study was 8 days, and the holding time for 90 percent of the samples did not exceed 15 days. Thus, the combination of small changes in concentrations for most analytes and the low holding times for most samples indicate that holding time between sample collection and extraction did not greatly affect pharmaceutical concentrations reported in this study.

Environmental Data

Quality-assurance and environmental data collected over the course of this study are described in the following sections.

Quality-Assurance Data

Blank and replicate data were collected in the field as part of quality-assurance data.

Blank Data

Sixty-nine field blanks were collected and analyzed during the study; 22 were collected prior to March 2006 and were analyzed for six of the seven analytes (all but carisoprodol), and 47 collected after March 2006 were analyzed for all seven analytes (table 17). Field blanks were prepared from laboratory-grade organic-free water and were processed and handled using the same methods WWTP effluent and streamwater samples.

Table 17. Pharmaceutical concentrations in field blank samples collected, 2004-09 (Excel format).

Three analytes were detected in field blanks: butalbital (two blanks ranging from 0.045 to 0.051 µg/L), oxycodone (two blanks, ranging from 0.15 to 0.73 µg/L), and metaxalone (seven blanks ranging from 0.068 to 1.0 µg/L). Detections in blanks were associated with effluent samples containing high pharmaceutical concentrations (>100 µg/L) and were attributed to the carryover of high concentrations to later samples in the same sample set. Concentrations in environmental samples within 10 times the concentrations in blanks which were collected during the same week were censored to a non-detection. Metaxalone blank contamination occurred in 20 percent of method blanks, therefore metaxalone concentrations below 3 µg/L (10 times the 90th percentile of concentrations in field blanks) were censored to a non-detection.

Replicate Data

Data on replicate samples are given in the data tables in the following section, and are listed just after the associated environmental sample. Analyses of 36 replicate samples yielded 85 paired-replicate detections of analytes, and 6 unpaired replicate detections (a detection in only one of the paired samples). All but one of the unpaired detections occurred for concentrations less than 0.2 µg/L. Median relative percent differences (RPDs) were similar among analytes, ranging from 3.9 percent for metaxalone to 13 percent for oxycodone. RPDs were somewhat greater for comparisons of low concentrations (9.9 percent for concentrations less than 0.2 µg/L) compared to comparisons of high concentrations (4.3 percent for concentrations > 10 µg/L).

Environmental Data for Pharmaceuticals in Wastewater-Treatment Plants, and in Streamwater and Reservoir Water

The following sections give information on the environmental data collected at the various WWTPs, streams, and reservoirs during this study.

Concentrations in Samples from National Survey of Wastewater-Treatment-Plant Effluent

Concentrations of pharmaceuticals in samples collected from the national survey of wastewater-treatment-plant effluent are listed in table 18. Five pharmaceuticals were detected in at least one effluent sample collected from the 23 WWTPs included in the national survey (fig. 1). Three pharmaceuticals (butalbital, carisoprodol, and oxycodone) were detected in more than 40 percent of these samples. Maximum concentrations ranged from less than 0.1 (diazepam) to 0.74 (butalbital) µg/L. Metaxalone and phendimetrazine were not detected in these effluent samples (table 18). Total pharmaceutical concentrations (equal to the sum of detected concentrations of all seven analytes for each sample) in samples from the 15 WWTPs that receive discharge from a hospital facility and the median total pharmaceutical concentrations in samples from the eight WWTPs without hospital discharge are given in figure 2.

Table 18. Pharmaceutical concentrations in samples of effluent from wastewater treatment plants in the national survey, 2006-09 (Excel format).

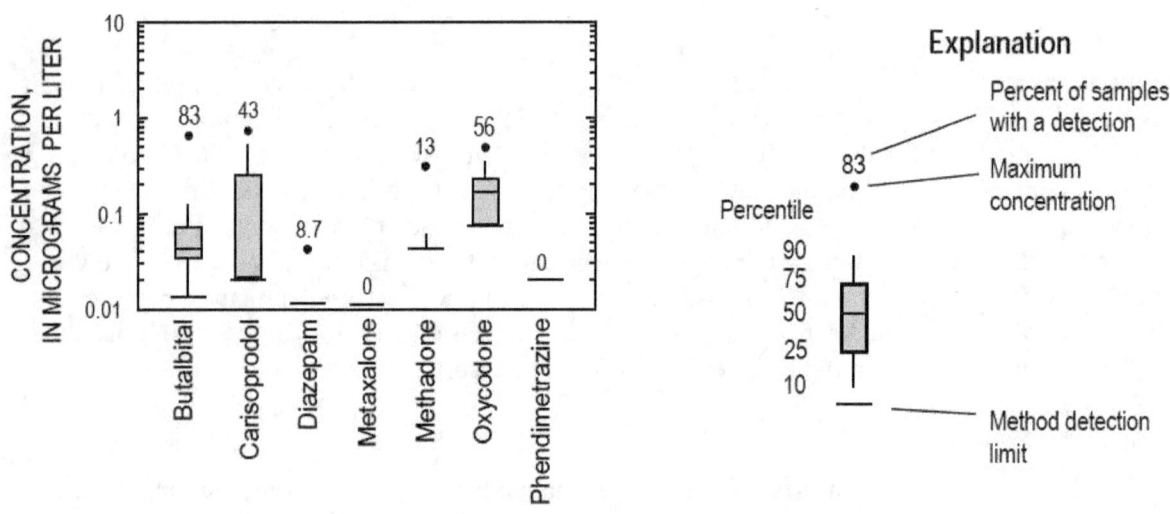

Figure 1. Concentrations of seven pharmaceutical compounds analyzed for in effluent from 23 wastewater treatment plants across the United States during 2006-09.

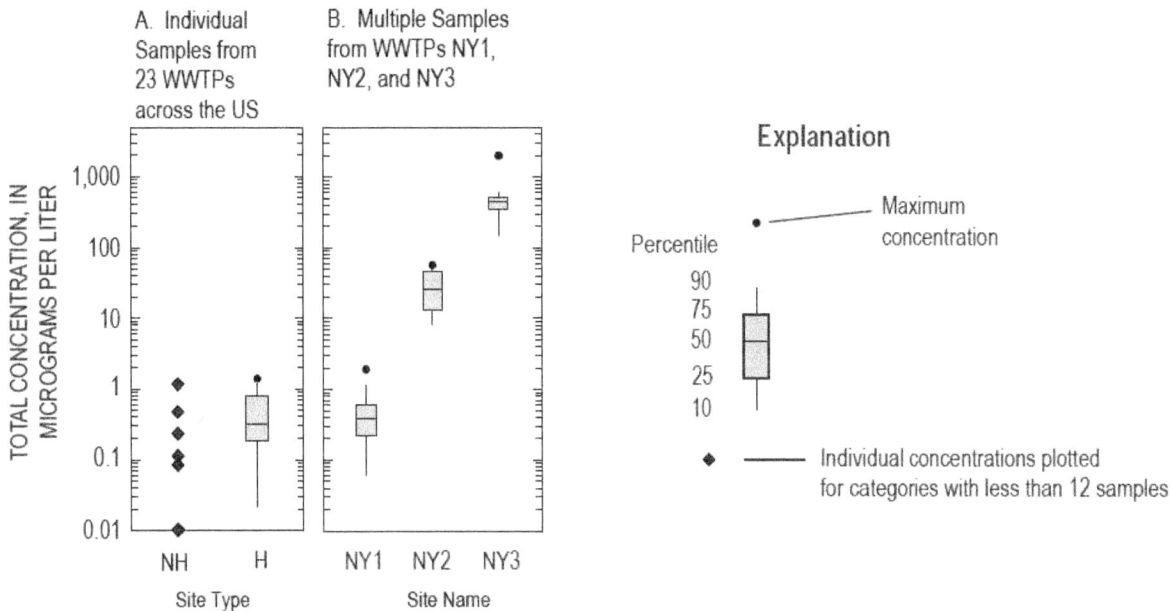

Figure 2. Total concentration of seven pharmaceutical compounds detected in effluent from wastewater treatment plants (WWTPs) (A) in individual samples from 23 plants across the United States 2006-09, and (B) in multiple samples from NY1, NY2, and NY3 in New York State, 2004-09.

[NH, WWTPs that do not receive discharges from hospitals; H, WWTPs that receive discharges from hospitals. Site NY1 does not receive discharge from a hospital or a PFF (pharmaceutical formulation facility). Site NY2 receives discharge from a hospital and approximately 20% of its discharge from a PFF. Site NY3 receives approximately 20% of its discharge from a PFF, but does not receive discharge from a hospital. For sites NY1, NY2, and NY3, only those samples with determinations for all seven analytes are included in the total concentration calculation.]

Concentrations in Effluent Samples from Wastewater-Treatment Plants NY1, NY2 and NY3

Concentrations of pharmaceuticals in samples collected from NY1 effluent are listed in table 19. Data on samples collected from NY2 effluent are listed in table 20, and data for samples collected from NY3 effluent are listed in table 21.

Table 19. Pharmaceutical concentrations in samples of effluent from wastewater treatment plant NY1, New York State, 2004-09 (Excel format).

Table 20. Pharmaceutical concentrations in samples of effluent from wastewater treatment plant NY2 in New York State, 2004-09 (Excel format).

Table 21. Pharmaceutical concentrations in samples of effluent from wastewater treatment plant NY3, in New York State, 2004-09 (Excel format).

Median concentrations of the five pharmaceuticals (butalbital, metaxalone, methadone, oxycodone, and phendimetrazine) most commonly detected in samples of NY3 effluent ranged from 0.5 to more than 400 µg/L; median concentrations of the four pharmaceuticals (butalbital, carisoprodol, diazepam, and oxycodone) most commonly detected in samples of NY2 effluent ranged from 0.74 to 11 µg/L (fig. 3). By contrast, median concentrations for the two pharmaceuticals (butalbital and oxycodone) most commonly detected in samples of NY1 effluent ranged from 0.10 to 0.19 µg/L (fig. 3). Maximum concentrations of oxycodone and metaxalone in samples of NY3 effluent were 1,700 and 3,800 µg/L, respectively, and maximum concentrations of three other pharmaceuticals (butalbital, methadone, and phendimetrazine) ranged from more than 40 to more than 400 µg/L. Two pharmaceuticals (butalbital and carisoprodol) had maximum concentrations greater than 40 µg/L in samples of NY2 effluent. Total concentrations of pharmaceuticals in samples of NY1, NY2, and NY3 effluent are given in figure 2.

The temporal variations in concentrations of carisoprodol and butalbital in samples of effluent from WWTP NY2 collected during 2004-09 are shown in figure 4. The temporal variations in concentrations of butalbital, oxycodone, metaxalone, and methadone in samples of effluent from WWTP NY3 collected during 2004-09 are shown in figure 5.

Concentrations in Samples of Streamwater Collected Downstream from WWTP Discharge Points of NY1, NY2, and NY3

Concentration data of pharmaceuticals in streamwater samples collected downstream from WWTP NY1 are listed in table 22. Concentration data of pharmaceuticals in streamwater samples collected downstream from WWTP NY2 are listed in table 23. Concentration data of pharmaceuticals in streamwater samples collected downstream from WWTP NY3 are listed in table 24.

Table 22. Pharmaceutical concentrations in samples of streamwater collected downstream from the discharge point of wastewater treatment plant NY1, in New York State, 2004-09 (Excel format).

Table 23. Pharmaceutical concentrations in samples of streamwater collected downstream from the discharge point of wastewater treatment plant NY2, in New York State, 2004-09 (Excel format).

Table 24. Pharmaceutical concentrations in samples of streamwater collected downstream from the discharge point of wastewater treatment plant NY3, in New York State, 2004-09 (Excel format).

The distribution of concentrations of each pharmaceutical in samples collected downstream from the discharge points of WWTPs NY1, NY2, and NY3 are shown in figure 6. The relation between the ratio of concentrations of butalbital and carisoprodol in streamwater collected downstream from the effluent discharge point to concentrations in NY2 effluent as a function of the percentage of streamflow consisting of NY2 effluent in samples collected downstream from NY2 is shown in figure 7 and provides a general indication of the combined effect of source concentrations and dilution on pharmaceutical concentrations in streamwater collected downstream from NY2. The temporal variations in concentrations of carisoprodol and butalbital in samples collected during 2004-09 downstream from the effluent discharge point of WWTP NY2 are shown in figure 4.

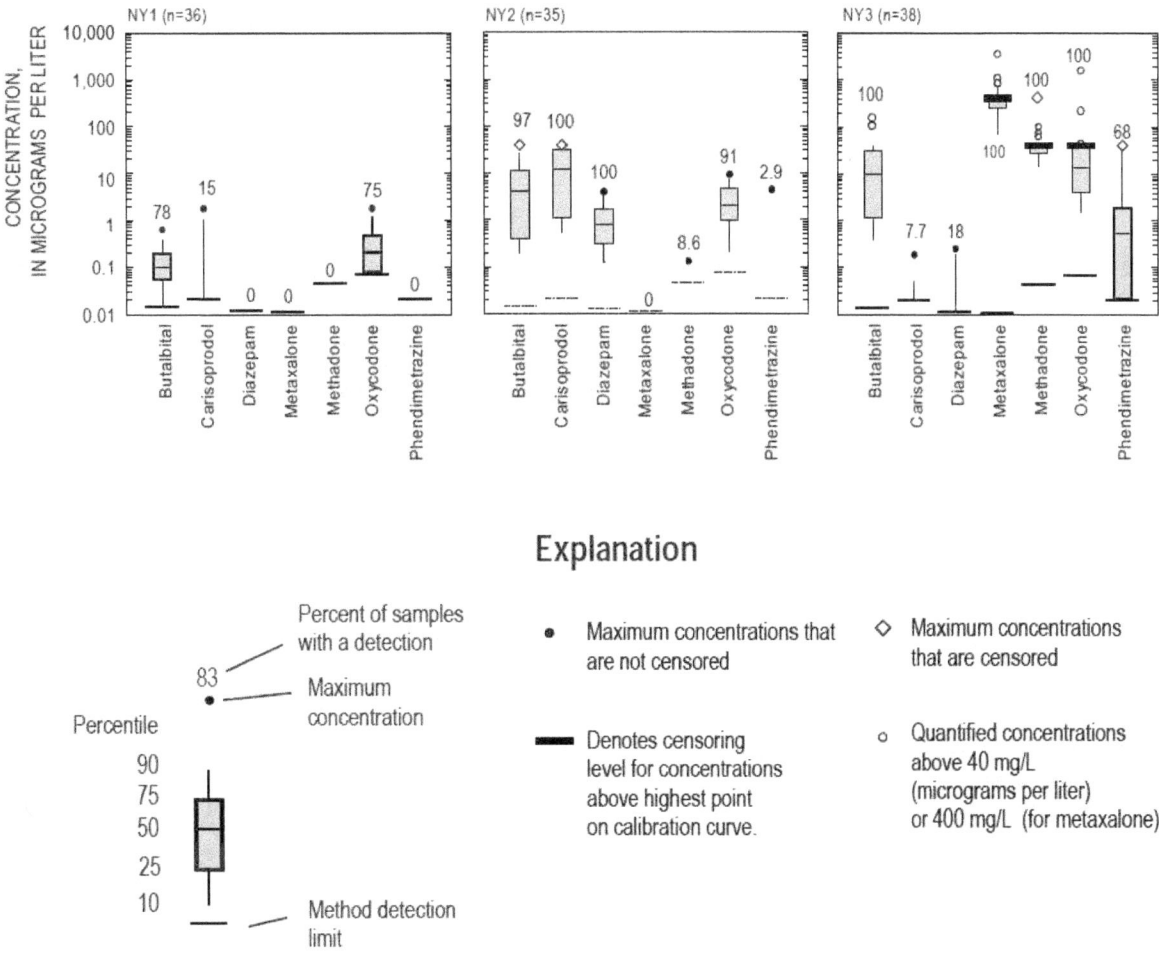

Figure 3. Concentrations of seven pharmaceuticals in samples of effluent from wastewater treatment plants (WWTPs) NY1, NY2, and NY3, New York State, during 2004-09.

[Site NY1 does not receive discharge from a hospital or a PFF (pharmaceutical formulation facility). Site NY2 receives discharge from a hospital and approximately 20% of its discharge from a PFF. Site NY3 receives approximately 20% of its discharge from a PFF, but does not receive discharge from a hospital. Numbers of samples for each site are indicated next to the site name. Twenty four (24) samples were analyzed for carisoprodol at each site. Boxplots for pharmaceuticals with censoring in more than 25% of the samples (including methadone, oxycodone and metaxalone in NY3 samples) were denoted by a boxplot truncated at the upper end with a bar.]

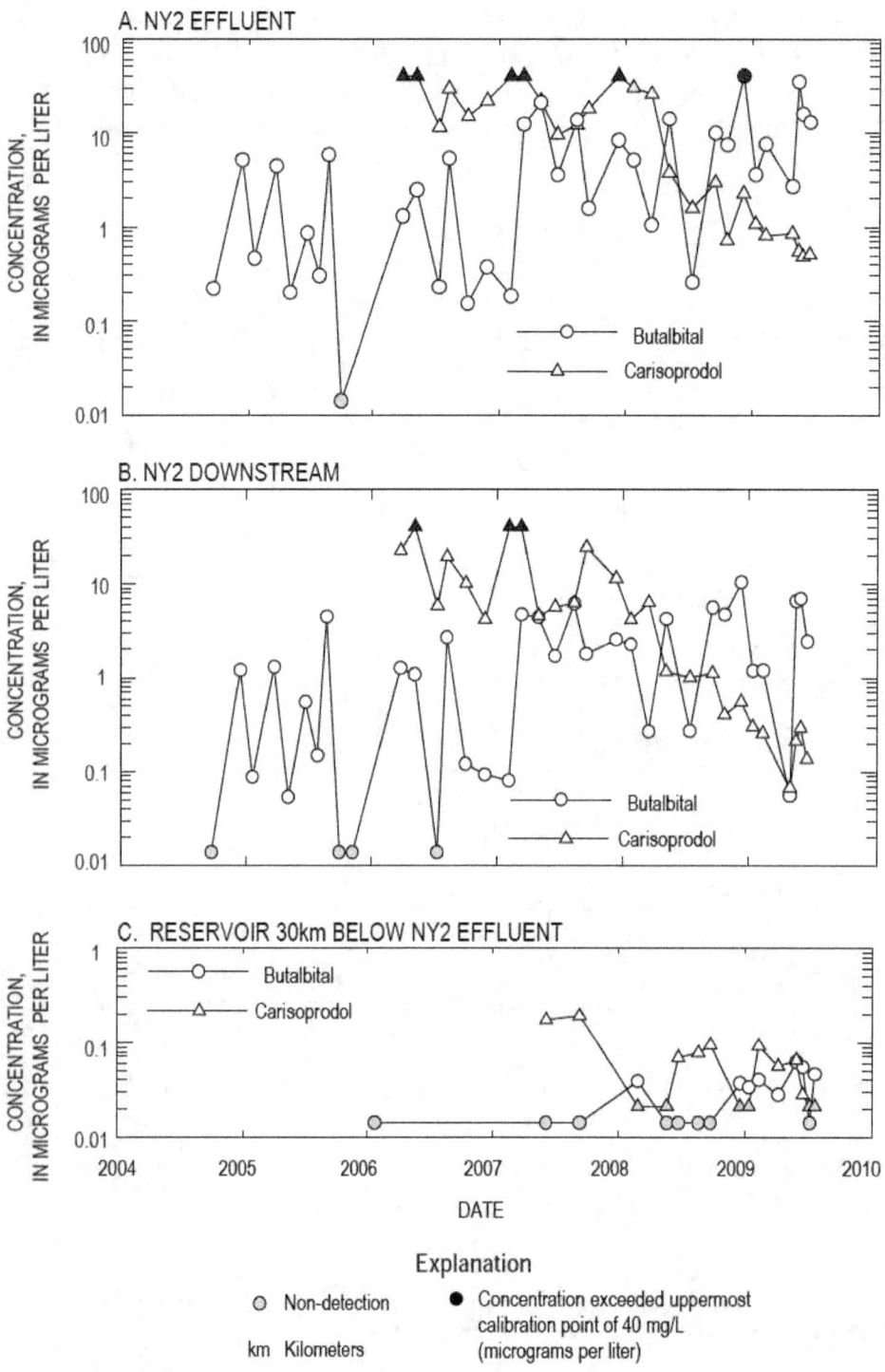

Figure 4. Concentrations of carisoprodol and butalbital in samples collected (A) from NY2 effluent, (B) from the NY2 effluent discharge point, and (C) at the reservoir site 30 kilometers downstream from the NY2 site in New York State, 2004-09.

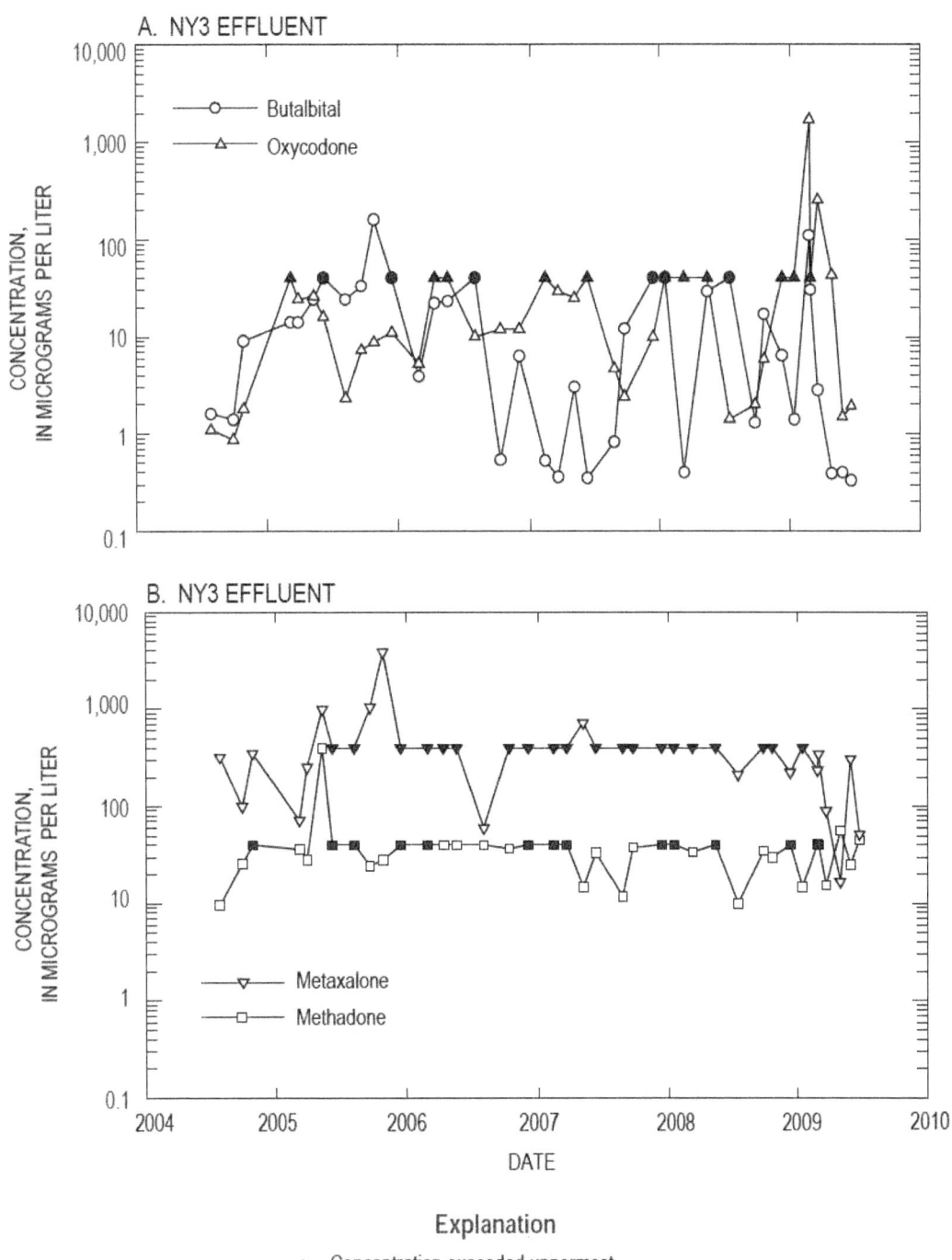

Figure 5. Concentrations of (A) oxycodone and butalbital, and (B) metaxalone and methadone in samples from NY3 effluent, 2004-09.

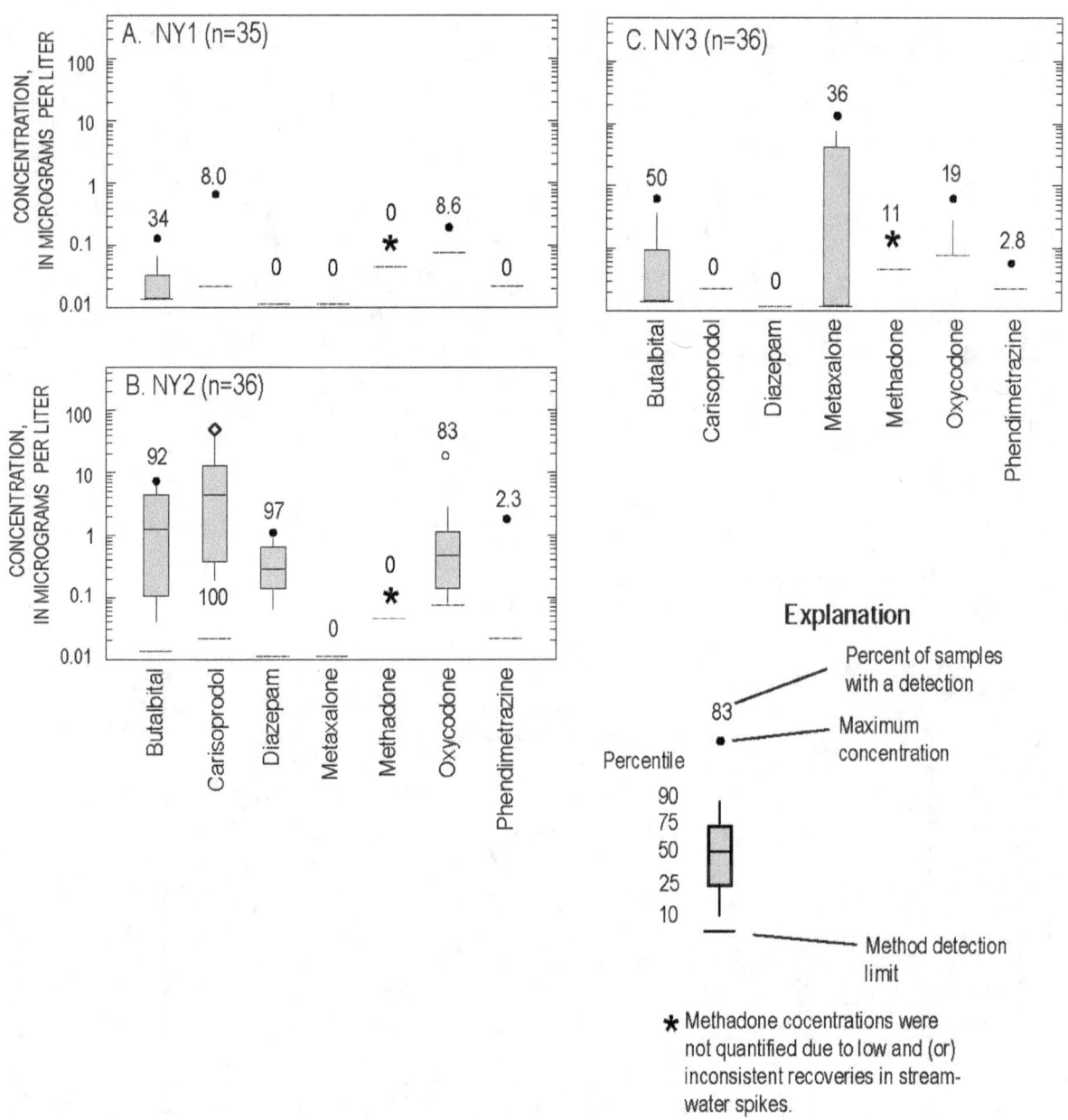

Figure 6. Concentrations of seven pharmaceuticals in samples collected downstream from the effluent discharge points of wastewater treatment plants NY1, NY2, and NY3 in New York State during 2004-09.

(Numbers of samples for each site are indicated next to the site name. Twenty-five samples collected downstream from the NY1 effluent discharge point were analyzed for carisoprodol, and 26 samples collected downstream from the NY2 and NY3 effluent discharge points were analyzed for carisoprodol.)

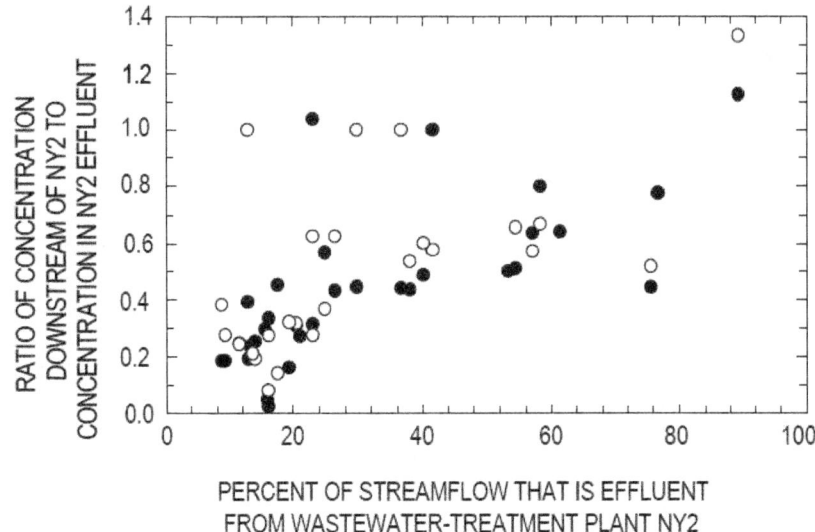

Figure 7. Ratio of the concentrations of butalbital and carisoprodol in streamwater downstream from NY2 effluent discharge point to the concentrations of the pharmaceutical in NY2 effluent as a function of the percentage of streamflow consisting of wastewater treatment plant NY2 effluent, 2004-09.

[<, less than; r refers to Spearman non-parametric correlation; p, probability value]

Concentrations in Samples of Streamwater Collected Upstream from WWTP NY1, NY2, and NY3 Discharge Points

Concentration data for pharmaceuticals in samples of streamwater collected upstream from the WWTP NY1 effluent discharge point are listed in table 25. Concentrations of pharmaceuticals in streamwater samples collected upstream from the WWTP NY2 effluent discharge point are listed in table 26, and concentrations of pharmaceuticals in samples of streamwater collected from the two sites upstream from the WWTP NY3 effluent discharge point are listed in table 27.

Table 25. Pharmaceutical concentrations in samples of streamwater collected upstream from the discharge point of wastewater treatment plant NY1, in New York State, 2004-09 (Excel format).

Table 26. Pharmaceutical concentrations in samples of streamwater collected upstream from the discharge point of wastewater treatment plant NY2, in New York State, 2004-09 (Excel format).

Table 27. Pharmaceutical concentrations in samples of streamwater collected at two sites upstream from the discharge point of wastewater treatment plant NY3, in New York State, 2004-09 (Excel format).

Only 3 pharmaceuticals included in this study (oxycodone, butalbital and metaxalone) were detected in samples collected in samples of streamwater collected upstream from the NY1, NY2, and NY3 effluent discharge points. Oxycodone was detected in 1 of 25 samples collected upstream from WWTP NY1 (0.26 µg/L). No other pharmaceutical was detected in samples collected upstream from WWTP NY1 (table 25). Butalbital was detected in 8 of 27 samples collected upstream from WWTP NY2; the maximum concentration is 0.069 µg/L. No other pharmaceutical was detected in 27 samples (17 samples for carisoprodol) collected upstream from WWTP NY2 (table 26). Oxycodone was detected in one sample (0.30 µg/L), butalbital was detected in 10 of 53 samples, and metaxalone was detected in 2 of 53 samples collected upstream from WWTP NY3 (table 27). Maximum concentrations ranged from 0.30 µg/L for oxycodone to 1.3 and 4.2 µg/L for butalbital and metaxalone, respectively. All but one butalbital detection in samples collected upstream from the WWTP NY3 effluent discharge point were less than 0.2 µg/L. No other pharmaceuticals were detected in 53 samples (30 samples for carisoprodol) collected upstream from WWTP NY3 (table 27).

Concentrations in Samples collected from Reservoirs and Additional Streams Downstream from NY2 Effluent Discharge Point

Concentration data for pharmaceuticals in reservoir samples can be found in table 28. Data for two sites, TD1 and TD2, that are located 1.2 miles (2.1 km) and 3.9 miles (6.6 km) downstream of the stream site where samples are collected below the NY2 effluent are found in table 29. In addition, data for site TD3, which is located on a site upstream of TD2 that does not receive any discharge from site NY2, can also be found in table 29. All the New York WWTP sites are located upstream of a New York Reservoir; sites NY1, NY2, and NY4-NY7 discharge to streams that are upstream of the RES01 site, site NY9 discharges to a stream that is upstream of the RES08 site, and sites NY3 and NY8 discharge to streams that are upstream of the RES09 site.

Table 28. Pharmaceutical concentrations in samples collected from New York reservoirs, 2006-09 (Excel format).

Table 29. Pharmaceutical concentrations in samples collected from sites below NY2 downstream site, in New York State, 2009 (Excel format).

With the exception of one reservoir (RES01), none of the pharmaceuticals were detected in the reservoir samples. Two pharmaceuticals (butalbital and carisoprodol) were detected in samples from RES01 (table 28), but no other pharmaceuticals included in the study were detected in samples from the RES01. Butalbital was detected in 8 of 16 samples from RES01, with a maximum concentration of 0.062 µg/L, but was not detected in 30 samples from 9 other reservoirs. (Replicate samples are not included in any calculations of percent detections in samples). Carisoprodol was detected in 9 of 15 samples from RES01 at a maximum concentration of 0.19 µg/L and was not detected in the 28 samples from 9 other reservoirs. The temporal trends in carisoprodol and butalbital at the RES01 site are shown in figure 4. Butalbital, carisoprodol, and diazepam were detected in most samples collected from sites TD1 and TD2 (table 29) but were not detected in samples from TD3.

Data on Qualitatively and Tentatively Identified Compounds

Ten additional pharmaceuticals or pharmaceutical degradates were qualitatively identified using authentic standards in at least two samples of the NY2 effluent collected during 2008-09 are listed in table 30. The pharmaceuticals quantified in this study in samples of NY2 effluent, along with an indication of the pharmaceuticals that are formulated by the PFF or marketed by the owner of the PFF that discharges to WWTP NY2 also are given in table 30. Additional pharmaceuticals that were tentatively identified in NY2 effluent samples are listed in table 31.

Eleven additional pharmaceuticals or pharmaceutical degradates that were qualitatively identified using authentic standards in at least two samples of effluent collected from NY3 during 2008-09 are listed in table 32. The pharmaceuticals quantified in this study in samples of NY3 effluent, along with an indication of the pharmaceuticals that are formulated by the PFF or marketed by the owner of the PFF that discharges to WWTP NY3 also are given in table 32. Additional pharmaceuticals that were tentatively identified in NY3 effluent samples are listed in table 33.

Table 30. Pharmaceuticals formulated by the pharmaceutical formulation facility or marketed by the owner of the facility discharging to wastewater treatment plant NY2 in New York State and quantified in samples of NY2 effluent or qualitatively identified in samples collected during 2008-09, or not identified in samples of NY2 effluent.

[Compounds with "na" for source were not identified as pharmaceutical products formulated at the pharmaceutical formulation facility, but were included because they were qualitatively identified and may represent a degradate of a pharmaceutical formulated at the facility. N indicates identified as manufactured at the facility or distributed by the corporation owning the facility (Daily Med, 2009); M, indicates distributed by the corporation owning the facility (Watson Pharmaceuticals, 2009); F, indicates formulated at the facility (Suzanne Fitzpatrick, Food and Drug Administration, written commun., 2009); na, not applicable]

Analyte	CASRN[a]	Source indicating production or marketing	Compound type/use
Pharmaceuticals quantified in this study			
Butalbital	77-26-9	N,M	Barbiturate
Carisoprodol	78-44-4	M	Muscle relaxant
Diazepam	439-14-15	N,M	Benzodiazepine
Oxycodone	76-42-6	F,N,M	Opioid
Pharmaceuticals qualitatively identified in samples using a standard, but not quantified[b]			
2-Ethyl-2-phenylmalonamide	7206-76-0	na	Primidone degradate
Bupropion	34841-39-9	F,N,M	Antidepressant
Diltiazem	42399-41-7	N,M	Calcium channel blocker
Hydrocodone	125-29-1	N,M	Opioid
Meprobamate	57-53-4	N,M	Antianxiety, carisoprodol degradate
Methocarbamol	532-03-6	N,M	Muscle relaxant
Methylphenidate	113-45-1	N,M	Psychostimulant (ritalin)
Phenobarbital	50-06-6	na	Metabolite of primidone
Primidone	125-33-7	N,M	Antiepileptic
Verapamil	52-53-9	N,M	Calcium channel blocker
Pharmaceuticals identified as formulated at the site, but not identified in effluent samples			
Acetaminophen	103-90-2	F	Analgesic
Anagrelide	68475-42-3	F	Platelet reducing agent
Colchicine	64-86-8	F	Rheumatic treatment
Gabapentin	60142-96-3	F	Gamma-aminobutyric acid analog
Hydrochlorothiazide	58-93-5	F	Thiazide diuretic
Ibuprofen	15687-27-1	F	Non-steroidal anti-inflammatory
Meperidine	57-42-1	F	Opioid
Metformin	657-24-9	F	Anti-diabetic
Quinidine	56-54-2	F	Antiarrhythmic
Sulindac	38194-50-2	F	Non-steroidal anti-inflammatory
Trazodone	19794-93-5	F	Piperazine antidepressant

[a] CAS Registry Numbers® is a Registered Trademark of the American Chemical Society. CAS recommends the verification of the CASRNs through CAS Client Services[SM].

[b] Compound qualitatively identified using criteria given in table 7 for samples collected between 2008-09.

Table 31. Tentatively identified compounds in samples of effluent from wastewater treatment plant NY2, New York State, 2004-09 (Excel format).

Table 32. Pharmaceuticals formulated by the pharmaceutical formulation facility (PFF) or marketed by the PFF owner discharging to wastewater treatment plant (WWTP) NY3 in New York State and quantified in samples of NY3 effluent or qualitatively identified in samples collected during 2008-09, or not identified in samples of NY3 effluent.

[Compounds with "na" for source were not identified as pharmaceutical products formulated at the pharmaceutical formulation facility, but were included because they were qualitatively identified and may represent a degradate of a pharmaceutical formulated at the facility. N indicates identified as manufactured at the facility or distributed by the corporation owning the facility (Daily Med, 2009); M, indicates distributed by the corporation owning the facility (Covidien Pharmaceuticals, 2009); F, indicates formulated at the facility (Suzanne Fitzpatrick, Food and Drug Administration, written commun., 2009); S, identified as formulated at the PFF by New York State FAIR report New York State Department of Environmental Conservation, 2009; na, not applicable]

Analyte	CASRN[a]	Source indicating Production or marketing	Compound type/use
Pharmaceuticals quantified in this study			
Butalbital	77-26-9	N,M	Barbiturate
Metaxalone	1665-48-1	S,N	Muscle relaxant
Methadone	76-99-3	F,N,M	Opioid
Oxycodone	76-42-6	N,M	Opioid
Phendimetrazine	634-03-7	N	Anorectic
Pharmaceuticals qualitatively identified in samples using a standard, but not quantified[b]			
Acetaminophen	103-90-2	F,S,N,M	Analgesic
Chlorpheniramine	132-22-9	N,M	Antihistamine
Codeine	76-57-3	F,N,M	Opioid
Dihydrocodeine	125-58-0	na	Opioid and opioid degradate
Fluoxetine	54910-89-3	F,N,M	SSRI antidepressant
Hydrocodone	125-29-1	F,N,M	Opioid
Meperidine	57-42-1	N,M	Opioid
Methylphenidate	113-45-1	N,M	Psychostimulant (ritalin)
O-Desmethyltramadol	73986-53-5	na	Tramadol degradate
Temazepam	846-50-4	F,N,M	Benzodiazepine
Tramadol	27203-92-5	F,N,M	Opioid
Pharmaceuticals identified as formulated at site, but not identified in samples			
Cocaine	50-36-2	M	Dopamine reuptake inhibitor
Dextroamphetamine	51-64-9	F	Amphetamine
Morphine	57-27-2	F	Opioid

[a] CAS Registry Numbers® is a Registered Trademark of the American Chemical Society. CAS recommends the verification of the CASRNs through CAS Client Services[SM].

[b] Compound qualitatively identified using criteria given in table 7 for samples collected between 2008-09.

Table 33. Tentatively identified compounds in samples of effluent from wastewater treatment plant NY3, in New York State, 2004-09 (Excel format).

Flow Data for Selected WWTP Effluent Samples and Streamwater Samples

WWTP Effluent discharge data for the dates that effluent samples were collected from NY1, NY2, and NY3 are provided in table 34. Streamflows measured at the time streamwater samples were collected from the sites downstream from NY1, NY2 and NY3 effluent discharge points are provided in table 35.

Table 34. Effluent discharge data for samples collected at wastewater treatment plants NY1, N2, and NY3 discharge points in New York State, 2004-09 (Excel format).

Table 35. Streamflow data for samples collected from downstream from wastewater treatment plants NY1, N2, and NY3 effluent discharge points, New York State, 2004-09 (Excel format).

Summary

Wastewater-treatment-plant effluents are a demonstrated source of pharmaceuticals to the environment. This report details the methods used to conduct a study to identify concentrations of seven pharmaceuticals in effluents from 26 WWTPs across the Nation, as well as streamwater and reservoirs. This report includes information on pharmaceuticals used or potentially used at the two pharmaceutical formulation facilities (PFFs) that provide substantial discharge to two of the WWTPs. The methods used to determine and quantify concentrations of seven pharmaceuticals (including opioids, muscle relaxants, and other pharmaceuticals) in filtered water samples are described. Data on method performance, including spike data and method detection limit analyses are provided and summarized. An estimate of precision is provided. Quality-assurance data for sample collection and handling are presented. Quantitative data are presented for the seven pharmaceuticals in water samples. Occurrence data are provided for 19 pharmaceuticals that were qualitatively identified in samples but were not quantified. Flow data at selected WWTP and streams also are included.

Between 2004-09, 35-38 effluent samples were collected from each of three WWTPs (wastewater treatment plants) in New York and analyzed for seven pharmaceuticals including opioids and muscle relaxants. Two WWTPs (NY2 and NY3) receive substantial flows (greater than 20 percent of plant flow) from PFFs and one (NY1) receives no PFF flow. Samples of effluents from 23 WWTP across the United States were analyzed once for these pharmaceuticals as part of a national survey. Maximum pharmaceutical effluent concentrations for the national survey and NY1 effluent samples were rarely (about 1 percent) greater than 1 µg/L. Four pharmaceuticals (methadone, oxycodone, butalbital and metaxalone) in samples of NY3 effluent had median concentrations ranging from 3.4 to greater than 400 µg/L. Maximum concentrations of oxycodone (1700 µg/L) and metaxalone (3800 µg/L) in samples from NY3 effluent exceeded 1000 µg/L. Three pharmaceuticals (butalbital, carisoprodol, and oxycodone) in samples of NY2 effluent had median concentrations ranging from 2 to 11 μg/L. These findings suggest that current manufacturing practices at these PFFs can result in pharmaceuticals concentrations from 10 to 1000 times higher than those typically found in WWTP effluents.

Publically available information on pharmaceuticals formulated at the PMFs is limited. Such information can be useful for designing studies that characterize the potential pharmaceutical source loadings to the environment from a PMF. Information provided in this report on pharmaceuticals formulated at PFFs that discharge to the two WWTPs is based on the a variety of sources, including direct FDA identification of selected pharmaceuticals formulated at the sites, a New York State Report indicating use of two pharmaceuticals at one of these sites, a web site operated by the U.S. National Institutes of Health (NIH) that identifies companies marketing or manufacturing pharmaceuticals, and manufacturers' web sites that listing the pharmaceuticals marketed by the owners of the two PFFs.

Acknowledgments

The authors thank the many USGS scientists and field technicians that provided assistance in site selection, collection, and processing of samples included in this study. Michelle Hladick and Michael Focazio provided useful comments on the draft manuscript. The authors also thank the New York State Department of Environmental Conservation for supporting the sampling in New York State. This project was conducted by the USGS Cooperative Water Program, New York State Department of Environmental Conservation, and the USGS Toxic Substances Hydrology Program. Elizabeth Nystrom formatted the text, tables and figures.

References Cited

Ashton, D., Hilton, M., and Thomas, K.V., 2004, Investigating the environmental transport of human pharmaceuticals to streams in the United Kingdom: Science of the Total Environment, v. 333, p. 167–184.

Brooks, B.W., Turner, P.K., Stanley, J.K., Weston, J.J., Glidewell, E.A., Foran, C.M., Slattery, M., La Point, T.W., and Huggett, D.B., 2003, Waterborne and sediment toxicity of fluoxetine to select organisms: Chemosphere v. 52, p. 135–142.

Bruchet, A., Hochereau, C., Picard, C., Decottignies, V., Rodrigues, J.M., and Janex-Habibi, M. L., 2005, Analysis of drugs and personal care products in French source and drinking waters: the analytical challenge and examples of application: Water Science and Technology, v. 52, p. 53–61.

Chang, H., Hu, J., and Shao, B., 2007, Occurrence of natural and synthetic glucocorticoids in sewage treatment plants and receiving river waters: Environmental Science and Technology, v. 41, p. 3462–3468.

Clara, M., Strenn, B., Gans, O., Martinez, E., Kreuzinger, N., and Kroiss, H., 2005, Removal of selected pharmaceuticals, fragrances and endocrine disrupting compounds in a membrane bioreactor and conventional wastewater treatment plants: Water Research, v. 39, p. 4,797–4,807.

Covidien, 2009, Covidien Pharmaceutical Products, accessed December 15, 2009, at http://pharmaceuticals.mallinckrodt.com/Products/ProductList.asp?UT=0.

Crane, M., Watts, C., and Boucard, T., 2006, Chronic aquatic environmental risks from exposure to human pharmaceuticals: Science of the Total Environment, v. 367, p. 23–41.

Daily Med, 2009, Current Medication Information, accessed December 15, 2009, at http://dailymed.nlm.nih.gov/dailymed/about.cfm.

Fick, J., Soderstrom, H., Lindberg, R., Phan, C., Tysklind, M., and Larsson, D., 2009, Contamination of surface, ground, and drinking water from pharmaceutical production: Environmental Toxicology and Chemistry, v. 28, p. 2522–2527.

Gaworecki, K.M., and Klaine, S.J., 2008, Behavioral and biochemical responses of hybrid striped bass during and after fluoxetine exposure: Aquatic Toxicology, v. 88, p. 207–213.

Glassmeyer, S.T., Furlong, E.T., Kolpin, D.W., Cahill, J.D., Zaugg, S.D., Werner, S.L., Meyer, M.T., and Kryak, D.D., 2005, Transport of chemical and microbial compounds from known wastewater discharges: Potential for use as indicators of human fecal contamination: Environmental Science and Technology, v. 39, no. 14, p. 5157–5169.

Heberer, T., and Feldmann, D., 2005, Contribution of effluents from hospitals and private households to the total loads of diclofenac and carbamazepine in municipal sewage effluents – modeling versus measurements: Journal of Hazardous Materials, v. 122, p. 211–218.

Hoerger, C., Dorr, B., Schlienger, C., and Straug, J., 2009, Environmental risk assessment for the galenical formulation of solid medicinal products at Roche Basle, Switzerland: Integrated Environmental Assessment and Management, v. 5, p. 331–337.

Karthikeyan, K.G., and Meyer, M.T., 2006, Occurrence of antibiotics in wastewater treatment facilities in Wisconsin, USA: Science of the Total Environment, v. 361, p. 196–207.

Kim, S.D., Cho, J., Kim, I.S., Vanderford, B.J., and Snyder, S.A., 2007, Occurrence and removal of pharmaceutical and endocrine disruptors in South Korean surface, drinking, and waste waters: Water Research, v. 41, p. 1013–1021.

Kolpin, D.W., Furlong, E.T., Meyer, M.T., Thurman, E.M., Zaugg, S.D., Barber, L.B., and Buxton, H.T., 2002, Pharmaceuticals, hormones, and other organic wastewater contaminants in

U.S. Streams, 1999–2000—A National Reconnaissance: Environmental Science and Technology, v. 36, p. 1,202–1,211.

Lamb, Ed, 2009, Top 200 drugs of 2008: Pharmacy Times, May 15, 2009, accessed November 3, 2009, at http://www.pharmacytimes.com/issue/pharmacy/2009/2009-05/RxFocusTop200Drugs-0509.

Larsson, D. G., de Pedro, C., Paxeus, N., 2007, Effluent from drug manufactures contains extremely high levels of pharmaceuticals: Journal of Hazardous Materials, v. 30, p. 751–755.

Lin, A., Yu, T., and Lin, C., 2008, Pharmaceutical contamination in residential, industrial, and agricultural waste streams: Risk to aqueous environments in Taiwan: Chemosphere, v. 74, p. 131–141.

Nentwig, G., 2007, Effects of pharmaceuticals on aquatic invertebrates. Part II: The antidepressant drug fluoxetine: Archives of Environmental Contamination and Toxicology, v. 52, p. 163–167.

New York State Department of Environmental Conservation, 2009, Fast Report on Significant Industries for SPDES Number 0029254: Attachment #1, January 20, 2009.

Paterson, G., and Metcalfe, C.D., 2008, Uptake and depuration of the anti-depressant fluoxetine by the Japanese medaka (Oryzias latipes): Chemosphere, v. 74, p. 125–130.

Phillips, P.J., Smith, S.G., Kolpin, D.W., Zaugg, S.D., Buxton, H.T., Furlong, E.T., Esposito, K., and Stinson, B., 2010, Pharmaceutical formulation facilities as sources of opioids and other pharmaceuticals to wastewater-treatment-plant effluents: Environmental Science and Technology, in press.

Pomati, F., Castiglioni, S., Zuccato, E., Fanelli, R., Vigetti, D., Rossetti, C., and Calamari, D., 2006, Effects of a complex mixture of therapeutic drugs at environmental levels on human embryonic cells: Environmental Science and Technology, v. 40, p. 2442–2447.

Quinn, B., Gagne, F., and Blaise, C., 2008, An investigation into the acute and chronic toxicity of eleven pharmaceuticals (and their solvents) found in wastewater effluent on the cnidarian, Hydra attenuate: Science of the Total Environment, v. 389, p. 306–314.

Rickert, D.A., 1990, Reporting of tentatively identified organic compounds: U.S. Geological Survey Office of Water Quality Technical Memorandum 90.11, accessed August 26 2009, at http://water.usgs.gov/admin/memo/historical/qw90.11Historical.txt.

Stanley, J.K., Ramirez, A.J., Chambliss, C.K., Brooks, B.W., 2007, Enantiospecific sublethal effects of the antidepressant fluoxetine to a model aquatic vertebrate and invertebrate: Chemosphere, v. 69, p. 9–16.

Ternes, T.A., Stumpf, M., Mueller, J., Haberer, K., Wilken, R.-D., and Servos, M., 1999, Behavior and occurrence of estrogens in municipal sewage treatment plants – I. Investigations in Germany, Canada, and Brazil: Science of the Total Environment, v. 225, p. 81–90.

U.S. Environmental Protection Agency, 2005, Guidelines establishing test procedures for the analysis of pollutants (App. B, Part 136, Definition and procedures for the determination of the method detection limit): U.S. Code of Federal Regulations, Title 40, revised as of July 1, 2005, p. 319–322.

Vieno, N., Tuhkanen, T., Kronberg, L., 2007, Elimination of pharmaceuticals in sewage treatment plants in Finland: Water Research, v. 41, p. 1001–1012.

Watkinson, A.J., Murby, E.J., Kolpin, D.W., and Costanzo, S.D., 2009, The occurrence of antibiotics in an urban watershed: from wastewater to drinking water: Science of the Total Environment, v. 407, p. 2711–2723.

Watson Pharmaceuticals, 2009, Interactive product database, accessed December 15, 2009, http://www.watson.com/products/product-database.asp.

Ying, G.G., Kooksana, R.S., and Kolpin, D.W., 2009, Occurrence and removal of pharmaceutically active compounds in sewage treatment plants with different technologies: Journal of Environmental Monitoring, v. 11, p. 1498–1505.

Zaugg, S.D., Smith, S.G., Schroeder, M.P., Barber, L.B., and Burkhardt, M.R., 2002, Methods of analysis by the U.S. Geological Survey National Water Quality Laboratory, Determination of wastewater compounds by polystyrene-divinylbenzene solid-phase extraction and capillary-column gas chromatography/ mass spectrometry: U.S. Geological Survey Water-Resources Investigations Report 2001–4186, p. 37.

For more information concerning this report, contact

Director
U.S. Geological Survey
New York Water Science Center
425 Jordan Road
Troy, NY 12180-8349
dc_ny@usgs.gov

or visit our Web site at:
http://ny.water.usgs.gov